SHARE A STORY

BEANS ON TOAST

Introduction

One of the best ways you can help
your children learn and learn to read
is to share books with them. Here's why:

• They get to know the **sounds**, **rhythms** and **words**
used in the way we write. This is different from how we
talk, so hearing stories helps children learn how to read.

• They think about the **feelings** of the characters
in the book. This helps them as they go about
their own lives with other people.

• They think about the **ideas** in the book. This helps
them to understand the world.

• Sharing books and listening to what your children
say about them shows your children that you care
about them, you care about what they think
and who they are.

Michael Rosen

Michael Rosen
Writer and Poet
Children's Laureate (2007-9)

For Carol and Peter

First published 1998 by Walker Books Ltd
87 Vauxhall Walk, London SE11 5HJ

This edition published 2011

2 4 6 8 10 9 7 5 3 1

© 1998 Paul Dowling
Concluding notes © CLPE 2011

The right of Paul Dowling to be identified as author/illustrator of this work has
been asserted by him in accordance with the Copyright, Designs and Patents Act 1988

This book has been typeset in Providence Sans Educational

Printed in China

British Library Cataloguing in Publication Data:
a catalogue record for this book is available from the British Library

ISBN 978-1-4063-3510-1

www.walker.co.uk

Beans
on Toast

Paul Dowling

WALKER BOOKS
AND SUBSIDIARIES
LONDON · BOSTON · SYDNEY · AUCKLAND

Beans on stalks

Beans on legs

Beans on racks

Beans on wheels

Beans on the road

Beans on cranes

Beans on the boil

Beans on tins

Beans on trucks

Beans on shelves

Beans on the counter

Beans on the way home

Beans on cooker

Beans on spoon

Beans on head

Beans on floor

Beans on toast

Sharing Stories

Sharing stories together is a pleasurable way to help children learn to read and enjoy books. Reading stories aloud and encouraging children to talk about the pictures and join in with parts of the story they know well are good ways to build their interest in books. They will want to share their favourite books again and again. This is an important part of becoming a successful reader.

Lots of people love to eat beans on toast! **Beans on Toast** is an enjoyable information book which helps children to understand where beans come from. Here are some ways you can share this book:

• As you read the book together, encourage children to predict what will happen next in the journey of the bean from the field to the plate.

• The repetition in the story of the beans helps children to learn to read the book quite quickly. Don't worry if the words they say aren't exactly the same as in the book at first. Re-reading the book together will help to build accuracy.

• If children are reading and get stuck on a word you can help them to guess what it might be from using the pictures, the meaning of the story and the first letter of the word. You can also read on and ask children to guess the missing word. If they're really stuck, just give them the word and carry on reading to keep it an enjoyable experience.

• Make beans on toast with a child, and invite them to draw each stage of the recipe to show someone else how to do it.

SHARE A STORY
A First Reading Programme
From Pre-school to School

Beginnings – 2 years+

- Look Out, Suzy Goose — Petr Horáček — Introduced by Michael Rosen
- Walking Through the Jungle — Julie Lacome — Introduced by Michael Rosen
- Hello, Goodbye — David Lloyd — Louise Voce — Introduced by Michael Rosen
- TEN IN THE BED — Penny Dale — Introduced by Michael Rosen
- THIS IS THE BEAR — Sarah Hayes — Helen Craig — Introduced by Michael Rosen
- The Big Wide-Mouthed Frog — Ana Martín Larrañaga — Introduced by Michael Rosen

Early Steps – 3 years+

- A New House for Mouse — Petr Horáček — Introduced by Michael Rosen
- The Train Ride — June Crebbin — Stephen Lambert — Introduced by Michael Rosen
- THE OTHER DAY I MET A BEAR — Russell Ayto — Introduced by Michael Rosen
- Old MacDonald Had a Farm — Jane Chapman — Introduced by Michael Rosen
- The Tiger and the Jackal — Vivian French — Alison Bartlett — Introduced by Michael Rosen
- Zed's Bread — Mick Manning — Brita Granström — Introduced by Michael Rosen

Next Steps – 4 years+

- The Hairy Toe — Daniel Postgate — Introduced by Michael Rosen
- The True Story of Humpty Dumpty — Sarah Hayes — Charlotte Voake — Introduced by Michael Rosen
- BEANS ON TOAST — Paul Dowling — Introduced by Michael Rosen
- Over in the Meadow — A Counting Rhyme — Louise Voce — Introduced by Michael Rosen
- Dog Blue — Polly Dunbar — Introduced by Michael Rosen
- Night-night, Knight And Other Poems — Michael Rosen — Sue Heap — Introduced by Michael Rosen

Taking Off – 5 years+

- "Have You Seen the Crocodile?" — Colin West — Introduced by Michael Rosen
- HANDA'S SURPRISE — Eileen Browne — Introduced by Michael Rosen
- The Ravenous Beast — Niamh Sharkey — Introduced by Michael Rosen
- One, Two, Flea! — Allan Ahlberg — Colin McNaughton — Introduced by Michael Rosen
- Dinosaurs' Day Out — Nick Sharratt — Introduced by Michael Rosen
- The Old Woman and the Red Pumpkin — Betsy Bang — Rachel Merriman — Introduced by Michael Rosen

Sharing the best books makes the best readers

WALKER BOOKS

www.walker.co.uk